school - école	2
travel - voyage	5
transport - transport	8
city - ville	10
landscape - paysage	14
restaurant - restaurant	17
supermarket - supermarché	20
drinks - boissons	22
food - alimentation	23
farm - ferme	27
house - maison	31
living room - salon	33
kitchen - cuisine	35
bathroom - chambre de bain	38
child's room - chambre d'enfant	42
clothing - vêtements	44
office - bureau	49
economy - économie	51
occupations - professions	53
tools - outils	56
musical instruments - instruments de musique	57
zoo - zoo	59
sports - sports	62
activities - activités	63
family - famille	67
body - corps	68
hospital - hôpital	72
emergency - urgence	76
Earth - terre	77
clock - horloge	79
week - semaine	80
year - année	81
shapes - formes	83
colours - couleurs	84
opposites - oppositions	85
numbers - nombres	88
languages - langues	90
who / what / how - qui / quoi / comment	91
where - où	92

Impressum
Verlag: BABADADA GmbH, Nedderfeld 112 , 22529 Hamburg
Geschäftsführer / Verlagsleitung: Harald Hof
Druck: Books on Demand GmbH, In de Tarpen 42, 22848 Norderstedt

Imprint
Publisher: BABADADA GmbH, Nedderfeld 112 , 22529 Hamburg, Germany
Managing Director / Publishing direction: Harald Hof
Print: Books on Demand GmbH, In de Tarpen 42, 22848 Norderstedt

school

école

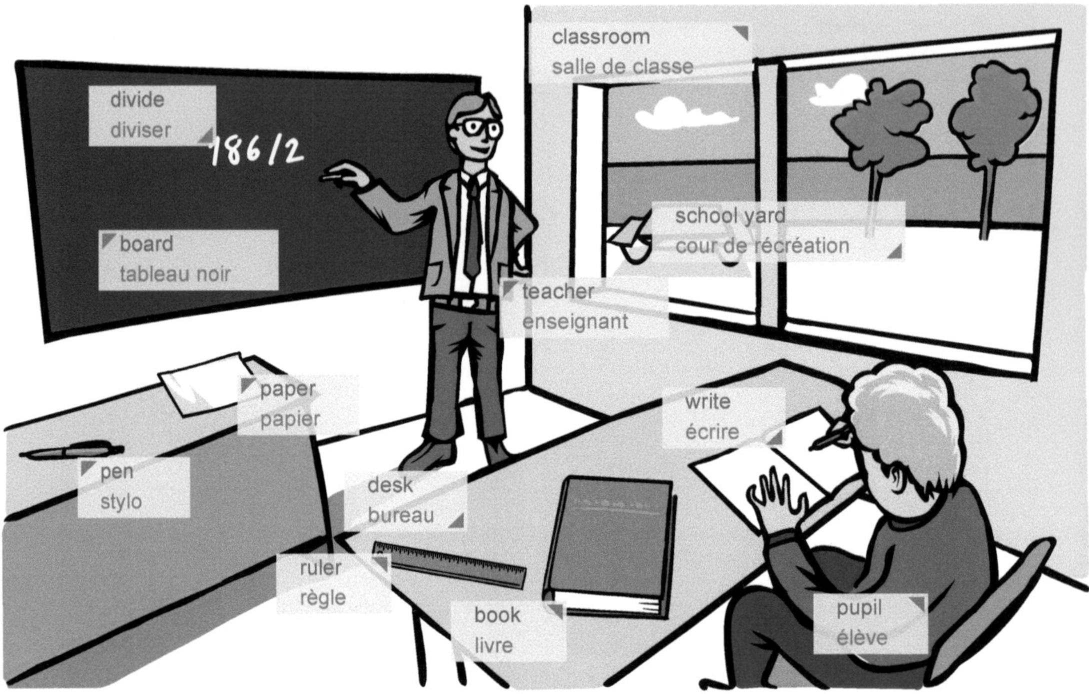
classroom
salle de classe
divide
diviser
186/2
board
tableau noir
school yard
cour de récréation
teacher
enseignant
paper
papier
write
écrire
pen
stylo
desk
bureau
ruler
règle
book
livre
pupil
élève

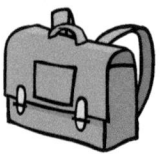

satchel

sac d'école

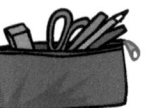

pencil case

trousse

pencil

crayon

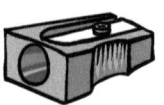

pencil sharpener

taille-crayon

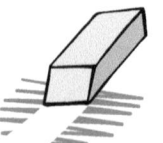

rubber

gomme

drawing pad

carnet à dessin

drawing

dessin

paintbrush

pinceau

paint box

boîte de peinture

scissors

ciseaux

glue

colle

exercise book

cahier d'exercices

homework

tâches

number

chiffre

2+2

add

additionner

subtract

soustraire

multiply

multiplier

calculate

calculer

letter

lettre

alphabet

alphabet

word

mot

text
....
texte

read
....
lire

chalk
....
craie

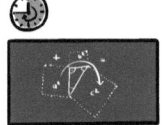

lesson
....
leçon

register
....
livre de classe

exam
....
examen

certificate
....
certificat

school uniform
....
uniforme scolaire

education
....
formation

encyclopedia
....
lexique

university
....
université

microscope
....
microscope

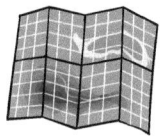

map
....
carte

waste-paper basket
....
corbeille à papier

travel
voyage

hotel
hôtel
Grand
hostel
auberge
ROOMS
CHANGE
bureau de change
bureau de change
car
voiture

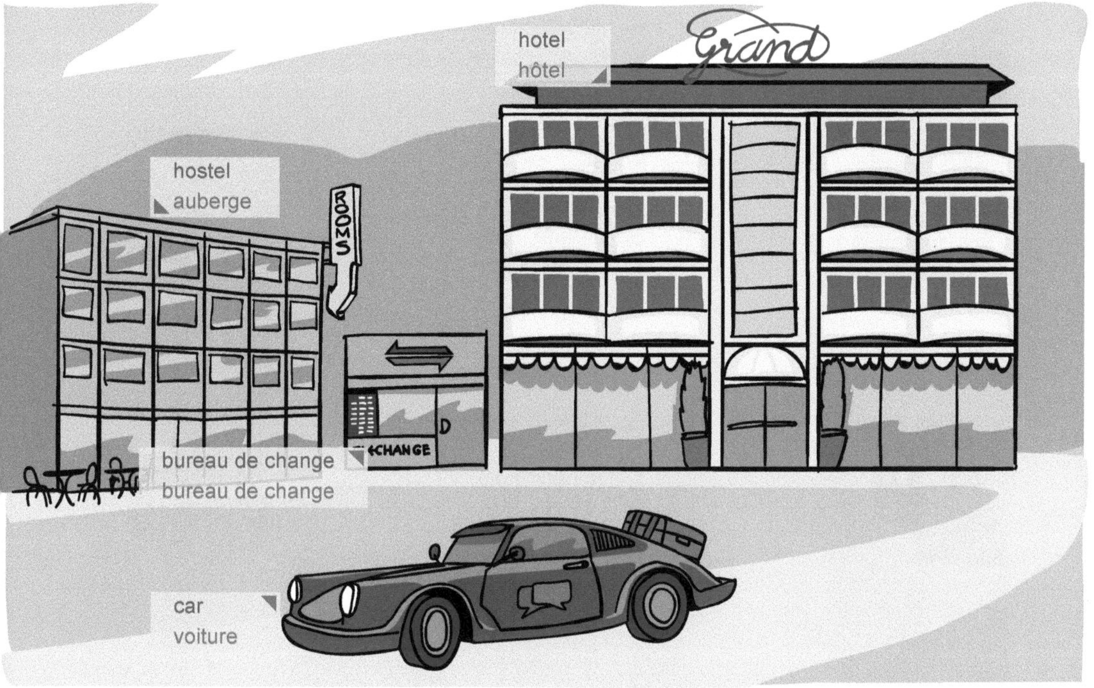

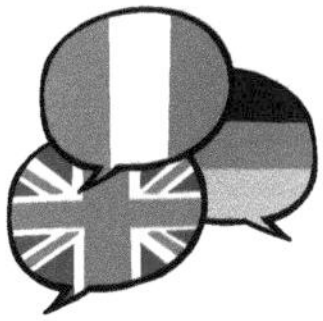

language

langue

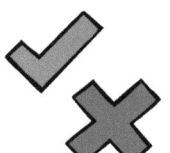

yes / no

oui / non

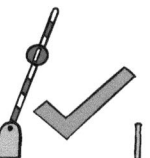

Okay

d'accord

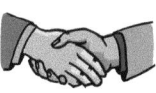

hello

Salut

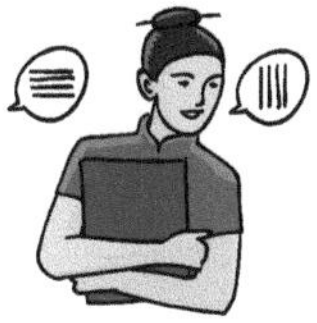

translator

interprète

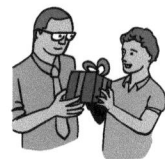

Thank you

merci

how much is...?

Combien coûte...?

I do not understand

Je ne comprends pas

problem

problème

Good evening!

Bonsoir!

Good morning!

Bonjour!

Good night!

Bonne nuit!

bye bye

Au revoir

direction

direction

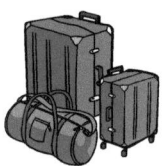

luggage

bagages

bag

sac

backpack

sac-à-dos

guest

hôte

room

pièce

sleeping bag

sac de couchage

tent

tente

tourist information

office de tourisme

beach

plage

credit card

carte de crédit

breakfast

petit-déjeuner

lunch

déjeuner

dinner

dîner

ticket

billet

lift

ascenseur

stamp

timbre

border

frontière

customs

douane

embassy

ambassade

visa

visa

passport

passeport

transport
transport

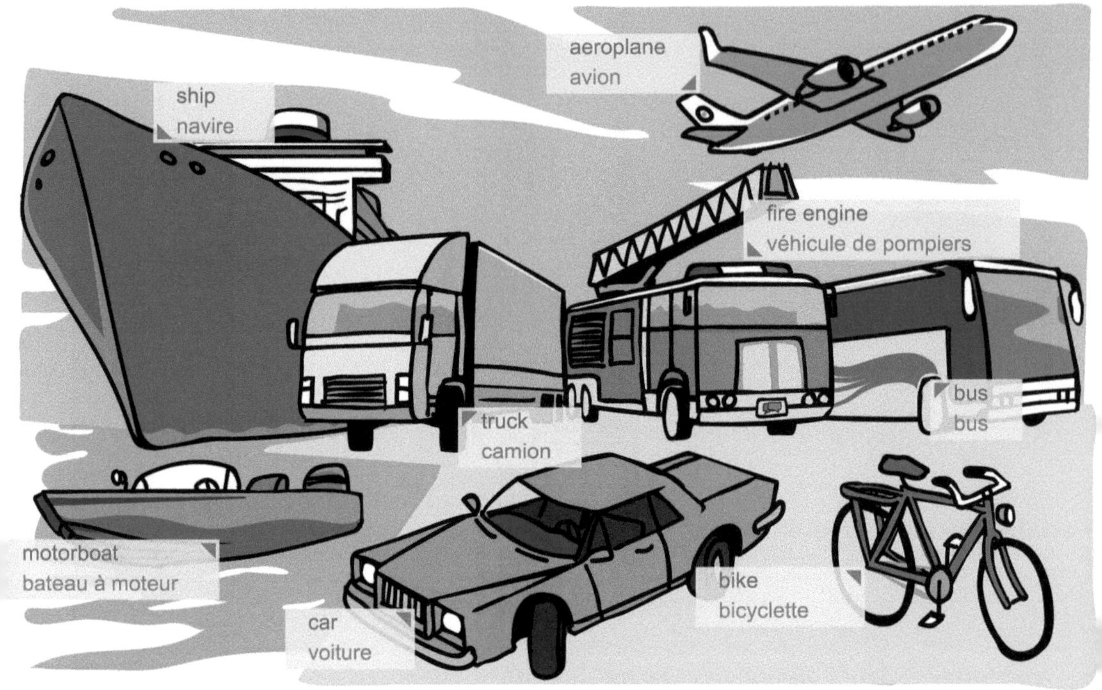
aeroplane
avion
ship
navire
fire engine
véhicule de pompiers
bus
bus
truck
camion
motorboat
bateau à moteur
bike
bicyclette
car
voiture

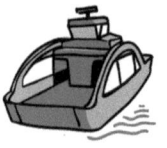

ferry

ferry

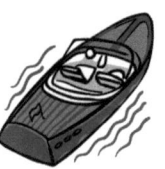

boat

barque

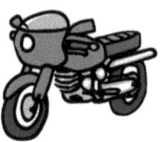

motorbike

moto

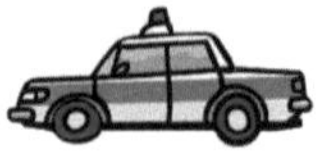

police car

voiture de police

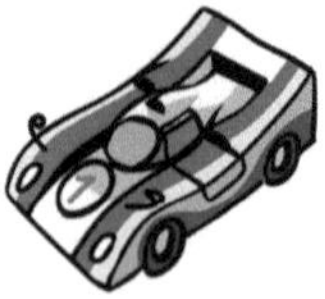

racing car

voiture de course

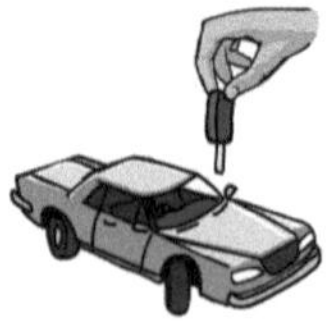

rental car

voiture de location

car sharing

autopartage

breakdown truck

dépanneuse

refuse truck

benne à ordures

motor

moteur

fuel

essence

petrol station

station d'essence

traffic sign

panneau indicateur

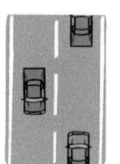

traffic

trafic

traffic jam

embouteillage

car park

parking

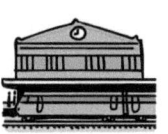

train station

gare

tracks

rails

train

train

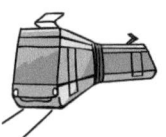

tram

tram

carriage

wagon

helicopter

hélicoptère

airport

aéroport

tower

tour

passenger

passager

container

container

carton

carton

cart

chariot

basket

corbeille

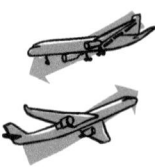

take off / land

décoller / atterrir

city

ville

village

village

city centre

centre-ville

house

maison

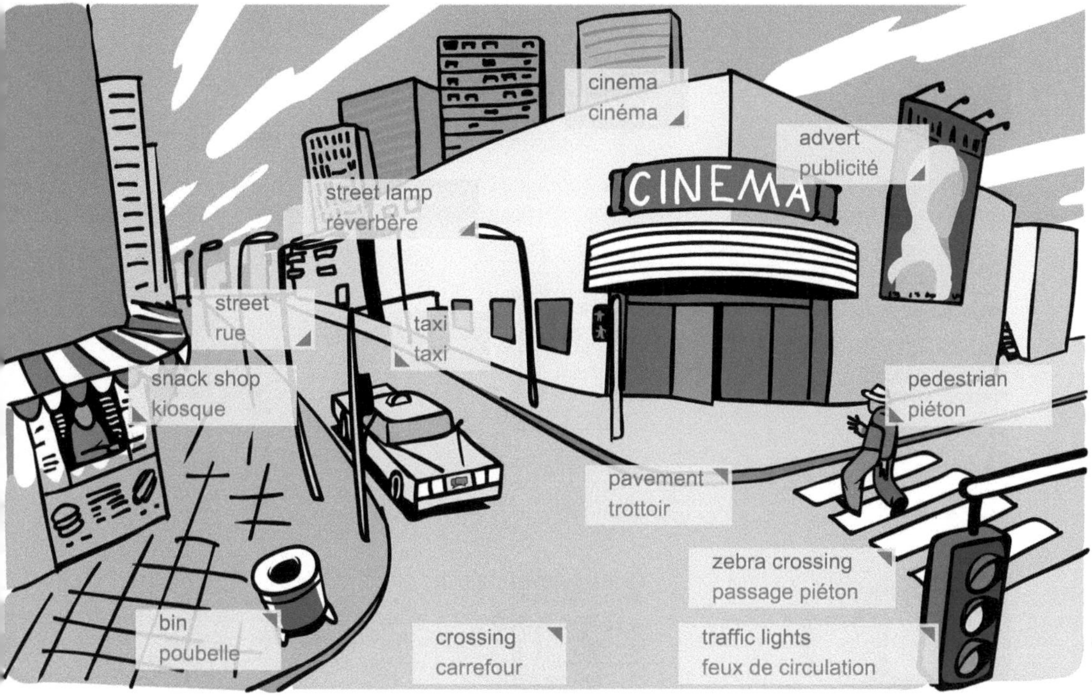

cinema
cinéma

advert
publicité

street lamp
réverbère

CINEMA

street
rue

taxi
taxi

snack shop
kiosque

pedestrian
piéton

pavement
trottoir

zebra crossing
passage piéton

bin
poubelle

crossing
carrefour

traffic lights
feux de circulation

hut

cabane

flat

appartement

train station

gare

town hall

mairie

museum

musée

school

école

university

université

bank

banque

hospital

hôpital

hotel

hôtel

pharmacy

pharmacie

office

bureau

book shop

librairie

shop

magasin

florist's

fleuriste

supermarket

supermarché

market

marché

department store

grand magasin

fishmonger's

poissonnerie

shopping centre

centre commercial

harbour

port

park

parc

bench

banque

bridge

pont

stairs

escaliers

underground

métro

tunnel

tunnel

bus stop

arrêt de bus

bar

bar

restaurant

restaurant

postbox

boîte à lettres

street sign

panneau indicateur

parking meter

parcomètre

zoo

zoo

swimming pool

réverbère

mosque

mosquée

farm

ferme

pollution

pollution

graveyard

cimetière

church

église

playground

aire de jeux

temple

temple

landscape

paysage

signpost
panneau indicateur

way
chemin

meadow
pré

stone
pierre

tree
arbre

hiker
randonneur

river
rivière

grass
herbe

flower
fleur

valley

vallée

hill

montagne

lake

lac

forest

forêt

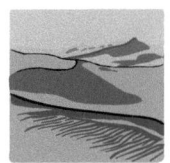

desert

désert

volcano

volcan

castle

château

rainbow

arc-en-ciel

mushroom

champignon

palm tree

palmier

mosquito

moustique

fly

mouche

ant

fourmis

bee

abeille

spider

araignée

beetle

scarabée

frog

grenouille

squirrel

écureuil

hedgehog

hérisson

hare

lapin

owl

chouette

bird

oiseau

swan

cygne

boar

sanglier

deer

cerf

moose

élan

dam

barrage

wind turbine

éolienne

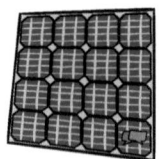

solar panel

panneau solaire

climate

climat

waiter
serveur

menu
menu

chair
chaise

soup
soupe

pizza
pizza

cutlery
services

tablecloth
nappe

starter
hors d'œuvre

main course
plat principal

dessert
dessert

drinks
boissons

food
alimentation

bottle
bouteille

fast food

fast-food

street food

plats à emporter

teapot

théière

sugar bowl

sucrier

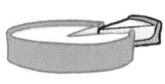

portion

portion

espresso machine

machine à expresso

high chair

chaise haute

bill

facture

tray

plateau

knife

couteau

fork

fourchette

spoon

cuillère

teaspoon

cuillère à thé

serviette

serviette

glass

verre

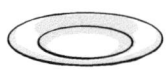

plate

assiette

soup plate

assiette à soupe

saucer

soucoupe

sauce

sauce

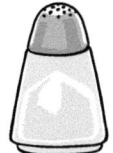

salt pot

salière

pepper mill

moulin à poivre

vinegar

vinaigre

oil

huile

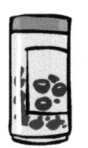

spices

épices

ketchup

ketchup

mustard

moutarde

mayonnaise

mayonnaise

supermarket
supermarché

special offer
offre promotionnelle
customer
client
dairy
produits laitiers
FOR
fruit
fruits
trolley
caddie

BUTCHERS

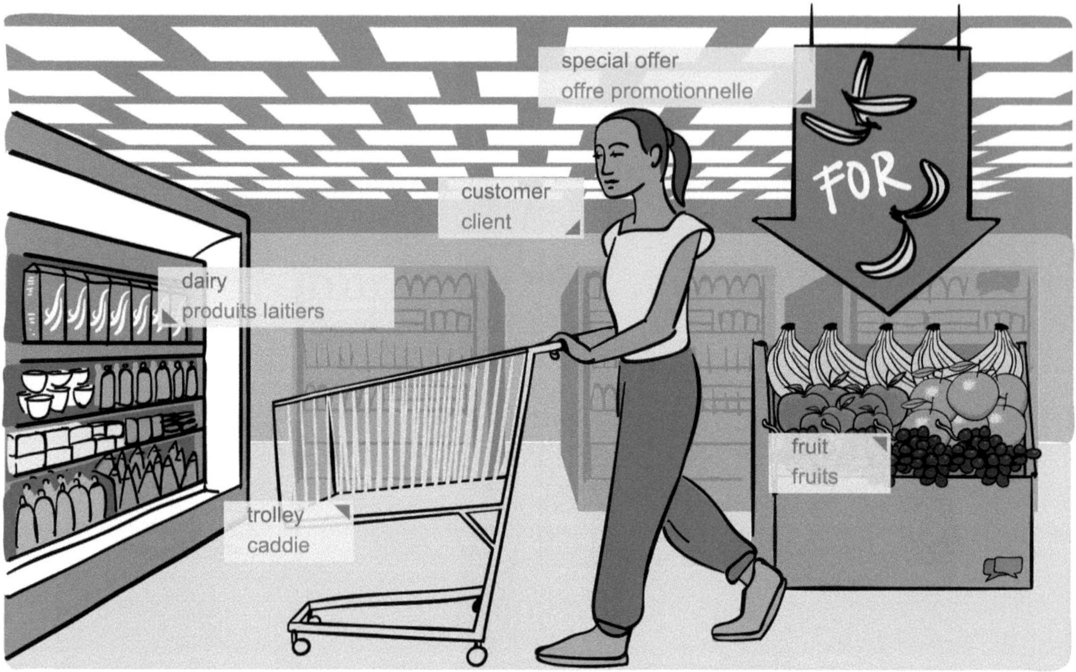

butcher´s
boucherie

BAKERY

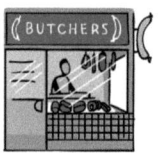

baker´s
boulangerie

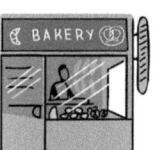

weigh
peser

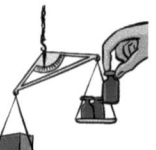

vegetables
légumes

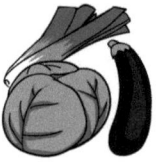

meat
viande

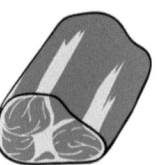

frozen food
aliments surgelés

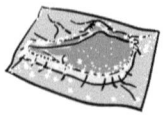

cold meat

charcuterie

tinned food

conserves

washing powder

poudre à lessive

sweets

bonbons

household products

articménagers

cleaning products

détergents

salesperson

vendeuse

till

caisse

cashier

caissier

shopping list

liste d'achats

opening hours

heures d'ouverture

wallet

portefeuille

credit card

carte de crédit

bag

sac

plastic bag

sac en plastique

water

eau

juice

jus de fruit

milk

lait

coke

coca

wine

vin

beer

bière

alcohol

alcool

cocoa

chocolat chaud

tea

thé

coffee

café

espresso

expresso

cappuccino

cappuccino

banana

banane

apple

pomme

orange

orange

melon

melon

lemon

citron

carrot

carotte

garlic

ail

bamboo

bambou

onion

oignon

mushroom

champignon

nuts

noisettes

noodles

pâtes

spaghetti

spaghettis

rice

riz

salad

salade

chips

frites

fried potatoes

pommes de terre rôties

pizza

pizza

hamburger

hamburger

sandwich

sandwich

cutlet

escalope

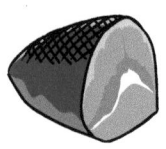

ham

jambon

salami

salami

sausage

saucisse

chicken

poulet

roast

rôti

fish

poisson

food - alimentation

porridge oats

flocons d'avoine

muesli

muesli

cornflakes

cornflakes

flour

farine

croissant

croissant

bread roll

petits-pains

bread

pain

toast

pain grillé

biscuits

biscuits

butter

beurre

curd

fromage blanc

cake

gâteau

egg

œuf

fried egg

œuf au plat

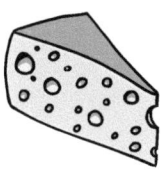

cheese

fromage

ice cream

glace

sugar

sucre

honey

miel

jam

confiture

chocolate spread

crème nougat

curry

curry

goat	cow	calf
chèvre	vache	veau

pig	piglet	bull
porc	porcelet	taureau

goose

oie

duck

canard

chick

poussin

hen

poule

cock

coq

rat

rat

cat

chat

mouse

souris

ox

bœuf

dog

chien

doghouse

chenil

garden hose

tuyau de jardin

watering can

arrosoir

scythe

faucheuse

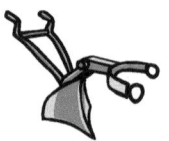

plough

charrue

sickle

faucille

hoe

pioche

pitchfork

fourche

axe

hache

wheelbarrow

brouette

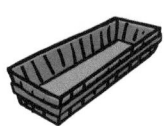

trough

cuve

milk can

pot à lait

sack

sac

fence

clôture

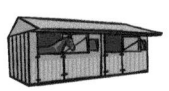

stable

étable

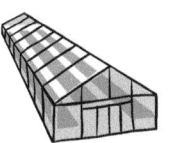

greenhouse

serre

soil

sol

seed

semences

fertilizer

engrais

combine harvester

moissonneuse-batteuse

farm - ferme

harvest

récolter

harvest

récolte

yams

igname

wheat

blé

soy

soja

potato

pomme de terre

corn

maïs

rapeseed

colza

fruit tree

arbre fruitier

cassava

manioc

cereals

céréales

house
maison

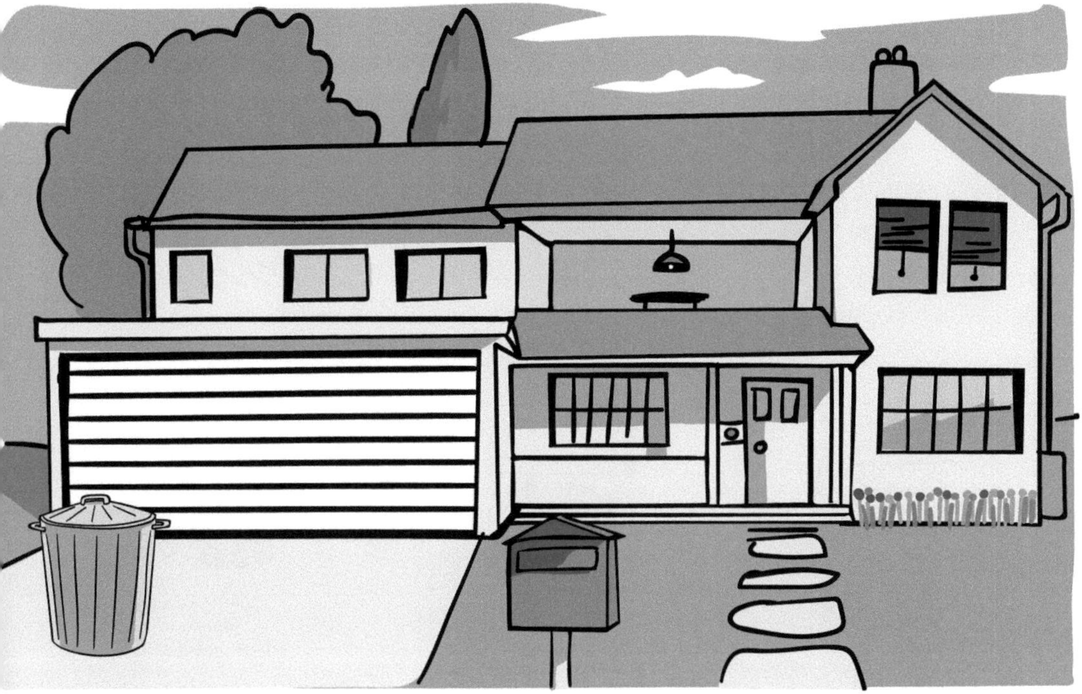

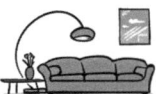

living room
salon

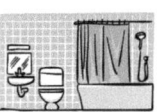

bathroom
chambre de bain

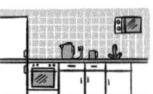

kitchen
cuisine

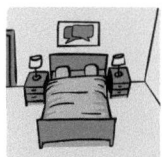

bedroom
chambre à coucher

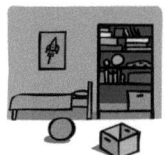

child's room
chambre d'enfant

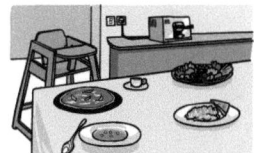

dining room
salle à manger

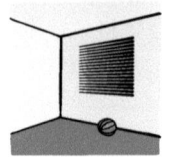

floor

sol

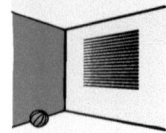

wall

mur

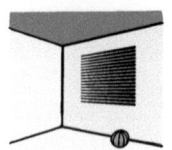

ceiling

plafond

cellar

cave

sauna

sauna

balcony

balcon

terrace

terrasse

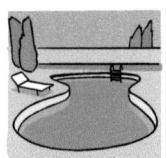

pool

piscine

lawn mower

tondeuse à gazon

sheet

fourre de duvet

bedspread

couette

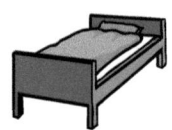

bed

lit

broom

balai

bucket

sceau

switch

interrupteur

carpet

tapis

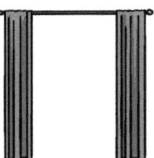

curtain

rideau

table

table

chair

chaise

rocking chair

chaise à bascule

armchair

fauteuil

book

livre

blanket

couverture

decoration

décoration

firewood

bois de chauffage

film

film

hi-fi equipment

chaîne hi-fi

key

clé

newspaper

journal

painting

peinture

poster

poster

radio

radio

notepad

bloc-notes

hoover

aspirateur

cactus

cactus

candle

bougie

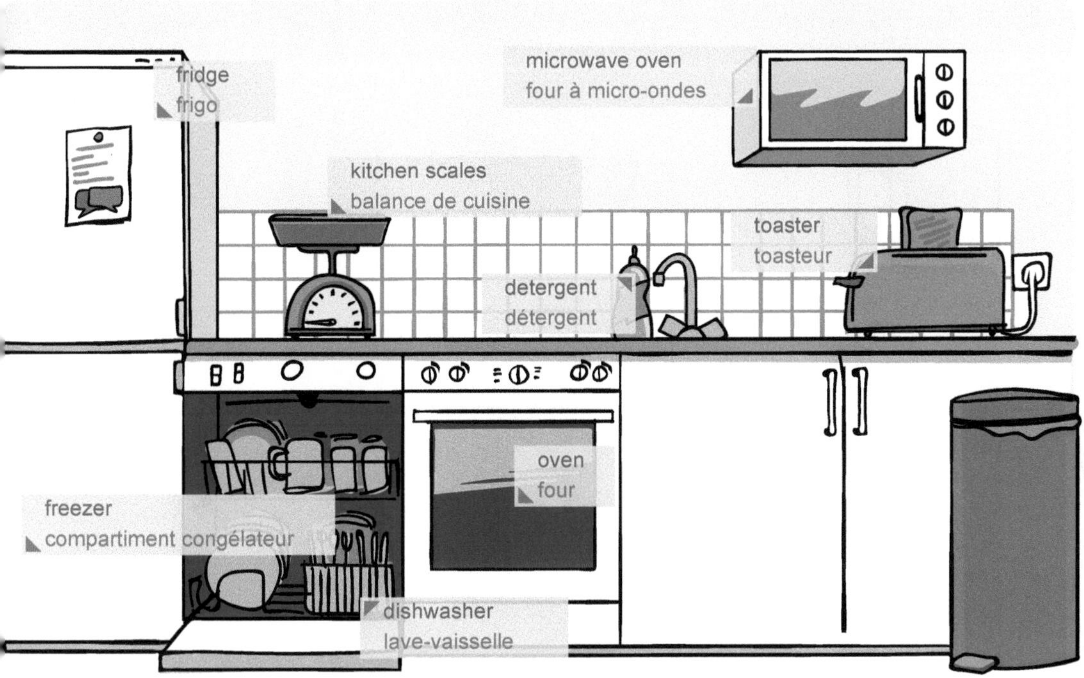

fridge
frigo

microwave oven
four à micro-ondes

kitchen scales
balance de cuisine

toaster
toasteur

detergent
détergent

oven
four

freezer
compartiment congélateur

dishwasher
lave-vaisselle

cooker
four

pot
casserole

cast-iron pot
marmite

wok / kadai
wok/kadai

pan
poêle

kettle
bouilloire électrique

steamer

cuiseur vapeur

baking tray

plaque de cuisson

crockery

vaisselle

mug

gobelet

bowl

bol

chopsticks

baguettes

ladle

louche

spatula

spatule

whisk

fouet

strainer

passoire

sieve

tamis

grater

râpe

mortar

mortier

barbecue

barbecue

open fire

cheminée

chopping board

planche à découper

rolling pin

rouleau à pâtisserie

corkscrew

tire-bouchon

can

boîte

can opener

ouvre-boîte

pot holder

maniques

sink

lavabo

brush

brosse

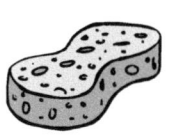

sponge

éponge

blender

mixeur

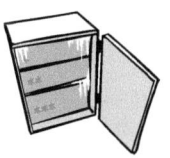

deep freezer

congélateur

baby bottle

biberon

tap

robinet

bathroom
chambre de bain

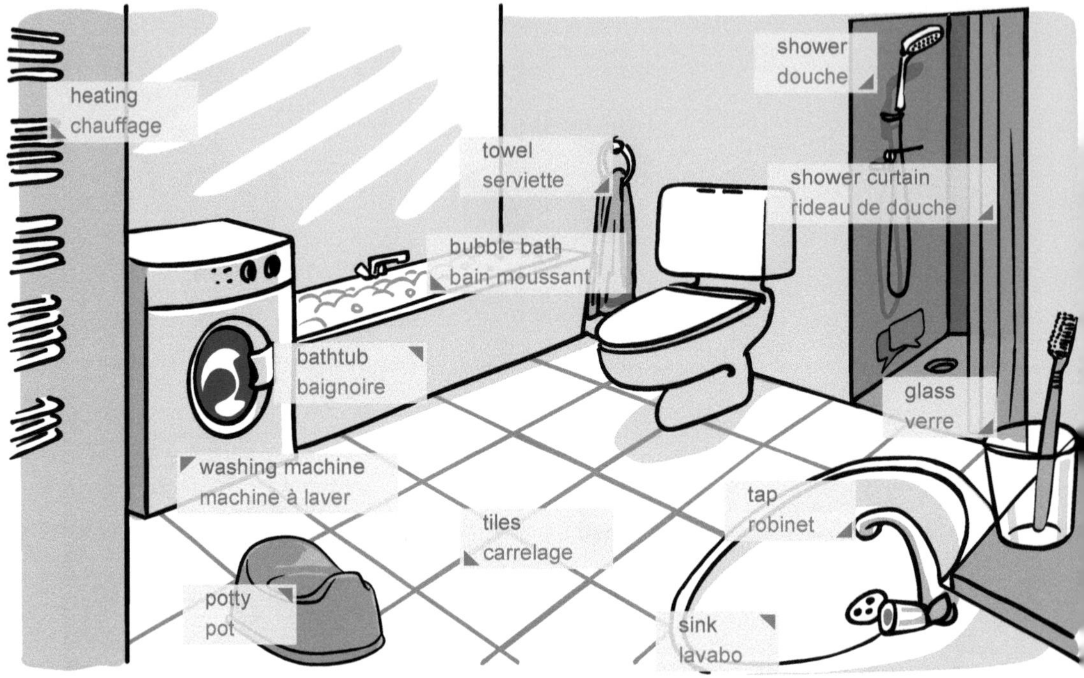
heating
chauffage
towel
serviette
shower
douche
shower curtain
rideau de douche
bubble bath
bain moussant
bathtub
baignoire
glass
verre
washing machine
machine à laver
tap
robinet
tiles
carrelage
potty
pot
sink
lavabo

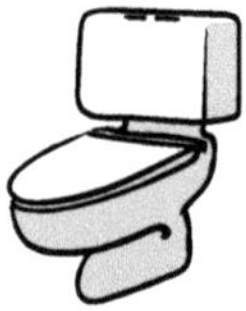

toilet

toilettes

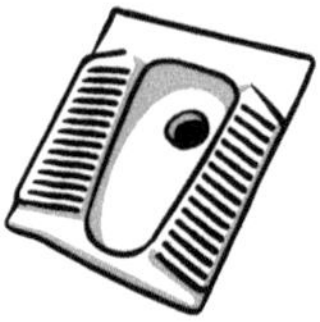

squat toilet

toilette à turque

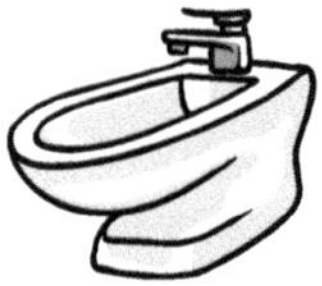

bidet

bidet

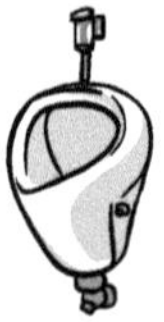

urinal

urinoir

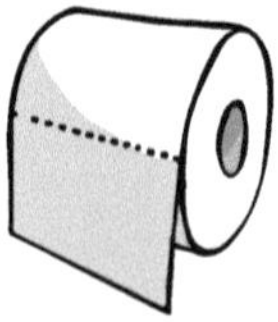

toilet paper

papier toilette

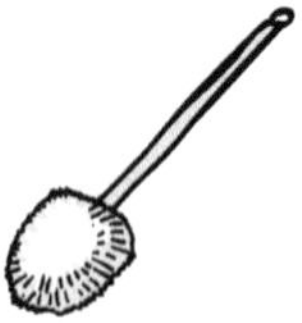

toilet brush

brosse à toilette

toothbrush

brosse à dents

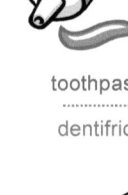

toothpaste

dentifrice

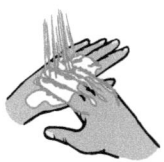

dental floss

fil dentaire

wash

laver

handheld shower

douche manuelle

douche

douche intime

basin

vasque

back brush

brosse dorsale

soap

savon

shower gel

gel douche

shampoo

shampooing

flannel

gant de toilette

drain

écoulement

cream

crème

deodorant

déodorant

mirror

miroir

hand mirror

miroir cosmétique

razor

rasoir

shaving foam

mousse à raser

aftershave

après-rasage

comb

peigne

brush

brosse

hair dryer

sèche-cheveux

hairspray

laque pour cheveux

makeup

fond de teint

lipstick

rouge à lèvres

nail varnish

vernis à ongles

cotton wool

ouate

nail scissors

coupe-ongles

perfume

parfum

bathroom - chambre de bain

washbag

trousse de toilette

stool

tabouret

weighing scale

balance

bathrobe

peignoir

rubber gloves

gants de nettoyage

tampon

tampon

sanitary towel

serviettes hygiéniques

chemical toilet

toilette chimique

child's room
chambre d'enfant

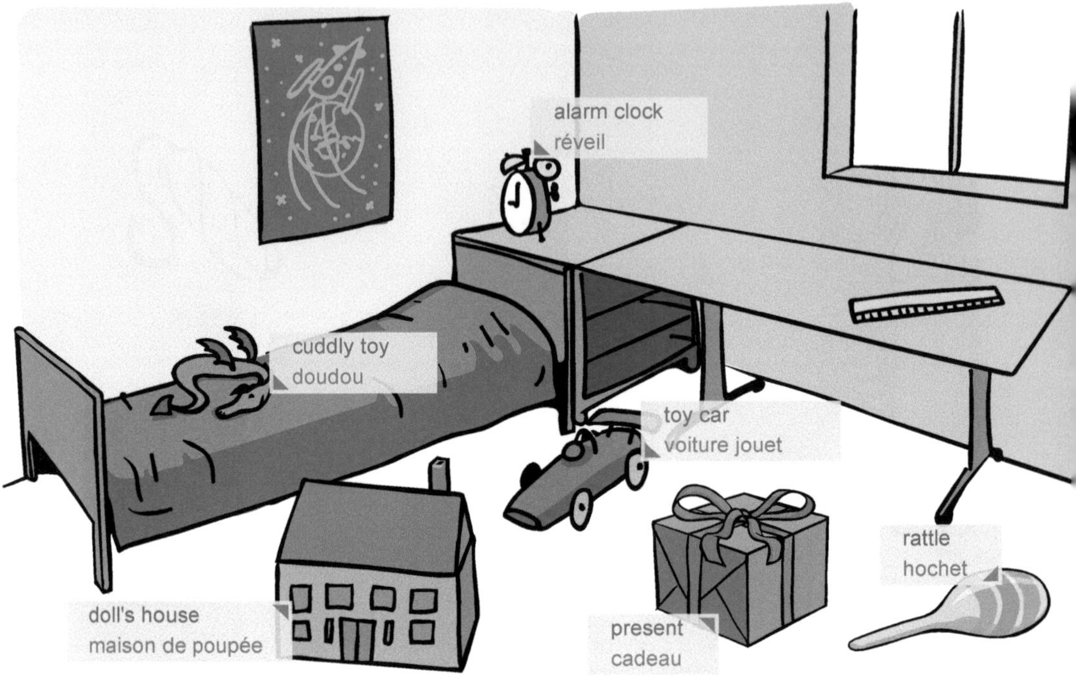

alarm clock
réveil
cuddly toy
doudou
toy car
voiture jouet
rattle
hochet
doll's house
maison de poupée
present
cadeau

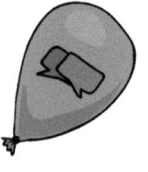

balloon

ballon

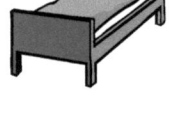

bed

lit

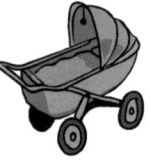

pram

poussette

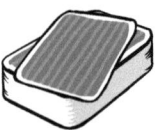

deck of cards

jeu de cartes

jigsaw

puzzle

SUPER MEGA

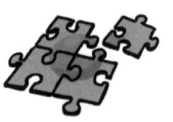

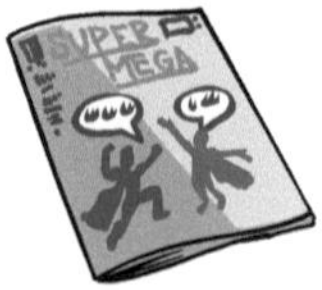

comic

bande dessinée

lego bricks

pièces lego

building blocks

blocs de construction

action figure

figurine

babygrow

grenouillère

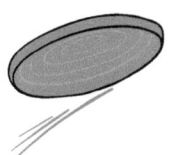

frisbee

frisbee

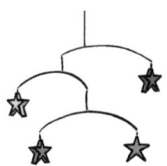

mobile

mobile

board game

jeu de société

dice

dé

model train set

train miniature

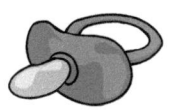

dummy

sucette

party

fête

picture book

livre d'images

ball

balle

doll

poupée

play

jouer

sandpit

bac à sable

swing

balançoire

toys

jouets

video game console

console de jeu

tricycle

tricycle

teddy bear

ours en peluche

wardrobe

armoire

clothing

vêtements

socks

chaussettes

stockings

bas

tights

collant

scarf
écharpe

belt
ceinture

umbrella
parapluie

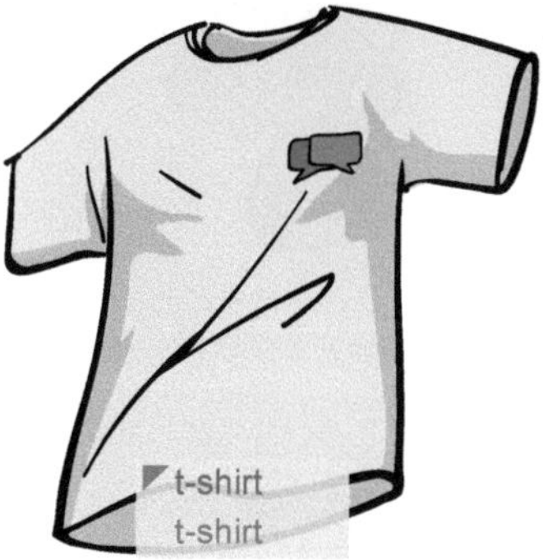

t-shirt
t-shirt

trainers
baskets

boots
bottes

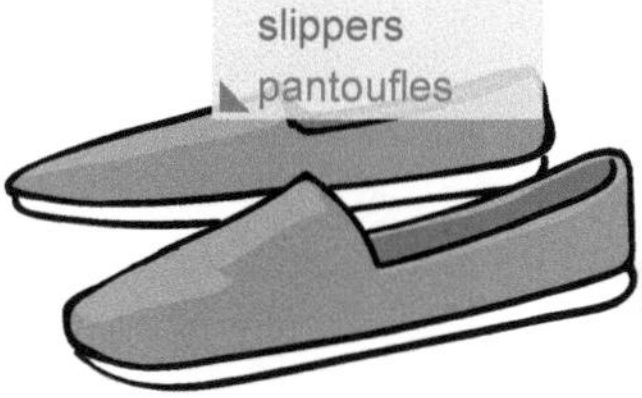

slippers
pantoufles

sandals
sandales

shoes
chaussures

rubber boots
bottes de caoutchouc

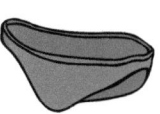
underpants
linge de corps

bra
soutien-gorge

vest
maillot de corps

body

body

trousers

pantalon

jeans

jean

skirt

jupe

blouse

chemisier

shirt

chemise

pullover

pull

hoodie

pull-over à capuche

blazer

veste

jacket

veste

coat

manteau

raincoat

imperméable

costume

costume

dress

robe

wedding dress

robe de mariée

clothing - vêtements

suit

costume

nightgown

chemise de nuit

pyjamas

pyjama

sari

sari

headscarf

foulard

turban

turban

burqa

burqa

kaftan

caftan

abaya

abaya

swimsuit

maillot de bain

trunks

costume de bain

shorts

cuissettes

tracksuit

tenue d'entraînement

apron

tablier

gloves

gants

button

bouton

glasses

lunettes

bracelet

bracelet

necklace

collier

ring

bague

earring

boucle d'oreille

cap

bonnet

coat hanger

cintre

hat

chapeau

tie

cravate

zip

fermeture éclair

helmet

casque

braces

bretelles

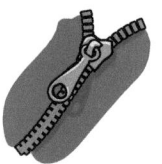

school uniform

uniforme scolaire

uniform

uniforme

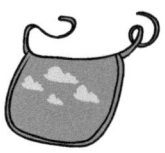

bib

bavoir

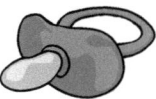

dummy

sucette

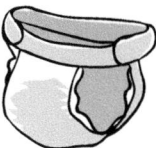

nappy

couche

office

bureau

server
serveur
filing cabinet
armoire d'archivage
printer
imprimante
paper
papier
monitor
écran
mouse
souris
desk
bureau
folder
classeur
keyboard
clavier
waste-paper basket
corbeille à papier
computer
ordinateur
chair
chaise

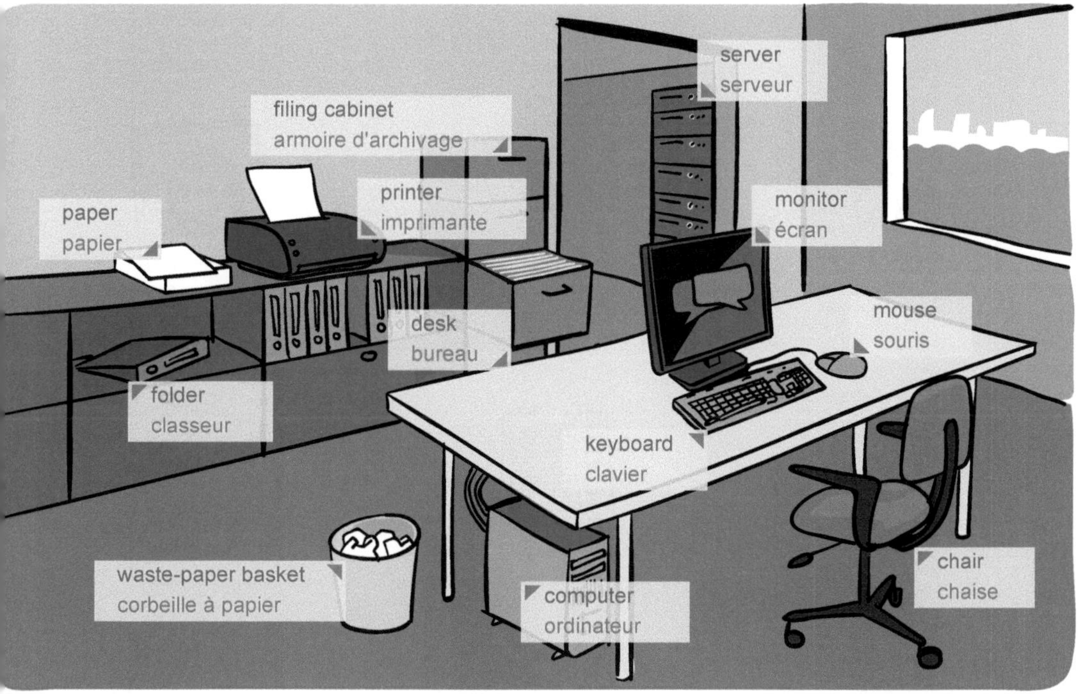

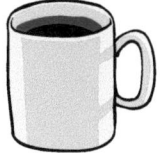

coffee mug

tasse à café

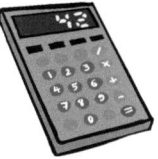

calculator

calculatrice

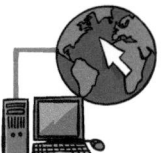

internet

internet

laptop

ordinateur portable

letter

lettre

message

message

mobile

portable

network

réseau

photocopier

photocopieuse

software

logiciel

telephone

téléphone

plug socket

prise

fax machine

fax

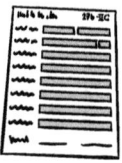

form

formulaire

document

document

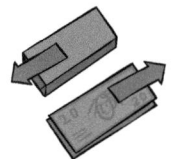

buy

acheter

pay

payer

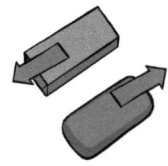

trade

marchander

money

monnaie

dollar

dollar

euro

euro

yen

yen

rouble

rouble

Swiss franc

franc suisse

renminbi yuan

renminbi yuan

rupee

roupie

cashpoint

distributeur automatique

bureau de change

bureau de change

gold

or

silver

argent

oil

pétrole

energy

énergie

price

prix

contract

contrat

tax

taxe

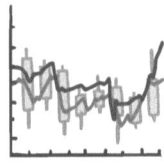

stock

action

work

travailler

employee

employé

employer

employeur

factory

usine

shop

magasin

police officer
agent de police

fireman
pompier

pilot
pilote

cook
cuisinier

doctor
médecin

gardener

jardinier

carpenter

menuisier

seamstress

couturière

judge

juge

chemist

chimiste

actor

acteur

bus driver

conducteur de bus

taxi driver

chauffeur de taxi

fisherman

pêcheur

cleaning lady

femme de ménage

roofer

couvreur

waiter

serveur

hunter

chasseur

painter

peintre

baker

boulanger

electrician

électricien

builder

ouvrier

engineer

ingénieur

butcher

boucher

plumber

plombier

postman

facteur

soldier

soldat

architect

architecte

cashier

caissier

florist

fleuriste

hairdresser

coiffeur

conductor

contrôleur

mechanic

mécanicien

captain

capitaine

dentist

dentiste

scientist

scientifique

rabbi

rabbin

imam

imam

monk

moine

clergyman

prêtre

tools
outils

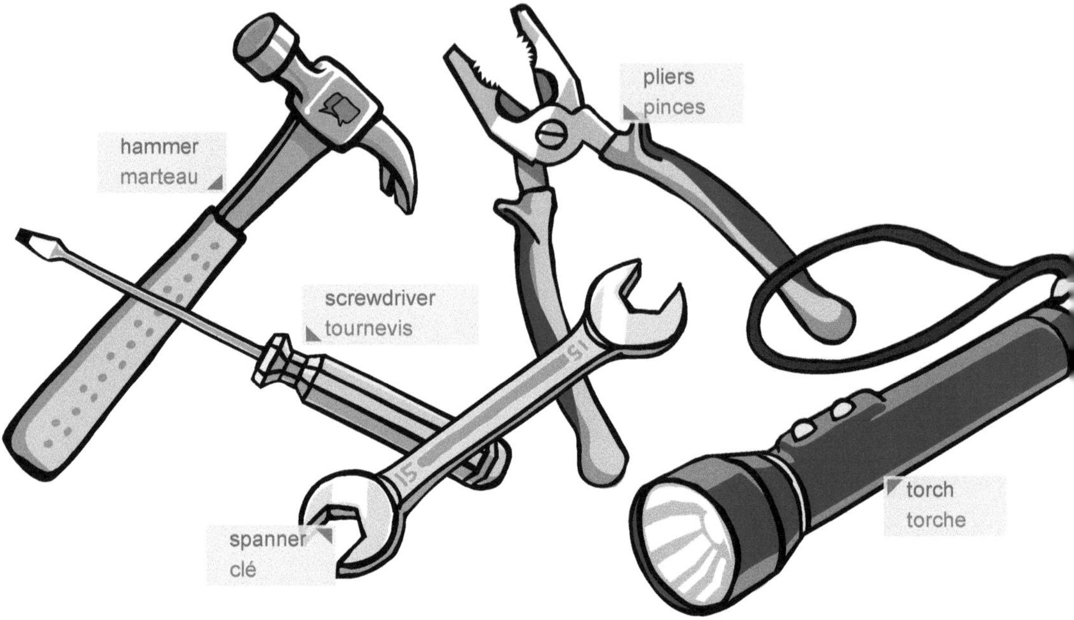
hammer
marteau
pliers
pinces
screwdriver
tournevis
spanner
clé
torch
torche

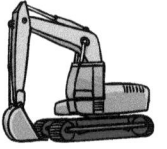

digger
pelleteuse

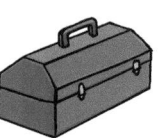

toolbox
boîte à outils

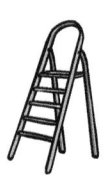

ladder
échelle

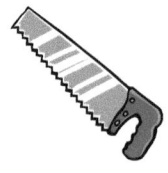

saw
scie

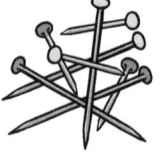

nails
clous

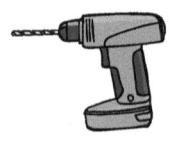

drill
perceuse

repair

réparer

shovel

pelle

Damn!

Mince!

dustpan

pelle

paint pot

pot de peinture

screws

vis

musical instruments
instruments de musique

loudspeaker
haut-parleur

drum kit
batterie

double bass
contrebasse

trumpet
trompette

guitar
guitare

piano

piano

violin

violon

bass

basse

timpani

timbales

drums

tambour

keyboard

piano électrique

saxophone

saxophone

flute

flûte

microphone

microphone

ZOO

ZOO

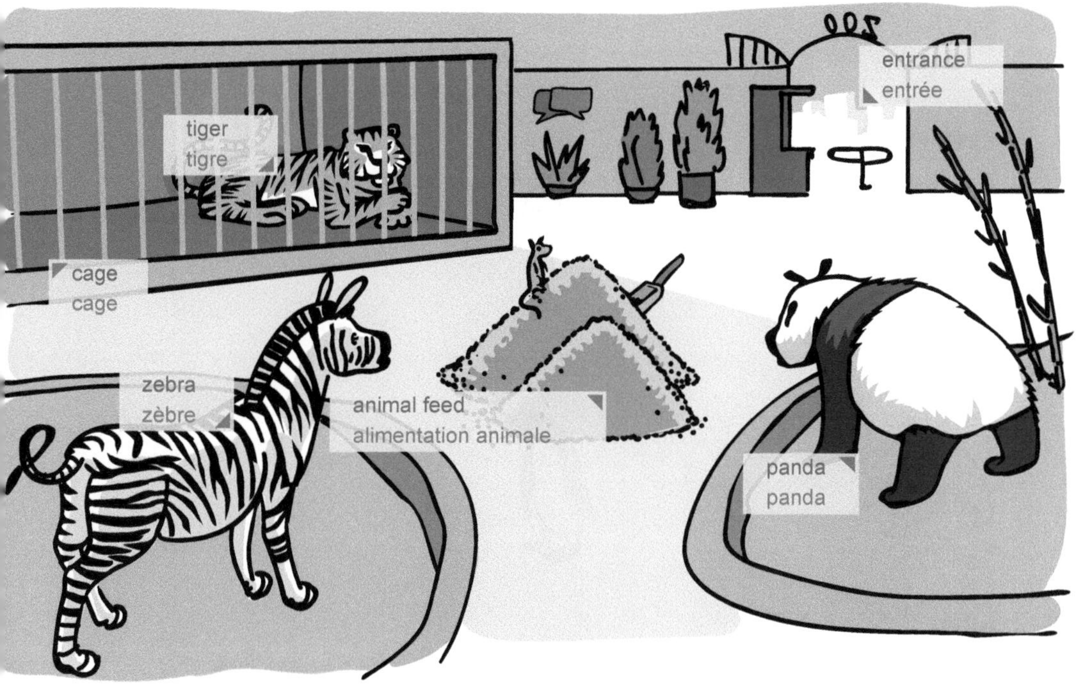
ZOO
entrance
entrée
tiger
tigre
cage
cage
zebra
zèbre
animal feed
alimentation animale
panda
panda

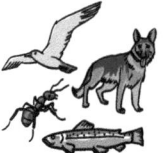

animals

animaux

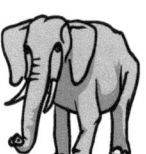

elephant

éléphant

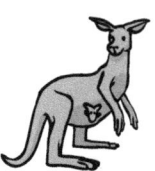

kangaroo

kangourou

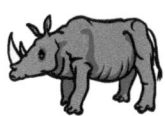

rhino

rhinocéros

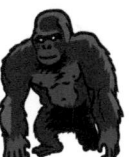

gorilla

gorille

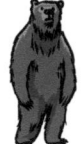

bear

ours

camel

chameau

ostrich

autruche

lion

lion

monkey

singe

flamingo

flamand rose

parrot

perroquet

polar bear

ours polaire

penguin

pingouin

shark

requin

peacock

paon

snake

serpent

crocodile

crocodile

zookeeper

gardien de zoo

seal

phoque

jaguar

jaguar

pony

poney

leopard

léopard

hippo

hippopotame

giraffe

girafe

eagle

aigle

boar

sanglier

fish

poisson

turtle

tortue

walrus

morse

fox

renard

gazelle

gazelle

American football
american Football

cycling
cyclisme

tennis
tennis

basketball
basket-ball

swimming
natation

boxing
boxe

ice hockey
hockey sur glace

football
football

badminton
badminton

athletics
athlétisme

handball
handball

skiing
ski

polo
polo

jump
sauter

hug
embrasser

laugh
rire

walk
marcher

sing
chanter

dream
rêver

pray
prier

kiss
faire la bise

write

écrire

draw

dessiner

show

montrer

push
pousser

give

donner

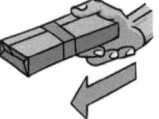

take

prendre

have
avoir

do
faire

be
être

stand
être debout

run
courir

pull
trier

throw
jeter

fall
tomber

lie
être couché

wait
attendre

carry
porter

sit
être assis

get dressed
s'habiller

sleep
dormir

wake up
se réveiller

look at

regarder

cry

pleurer

stroke

caresser

comb

peigner

talk

parler

understand

comprendre

ask

demander

listen

écouter

drink

boire

eat

manger

tidy up

ranger

love

aimer

cook

cuire

drive

conduire

fly

voler

sail

faire de la voile

calculate

calculer

read

lire

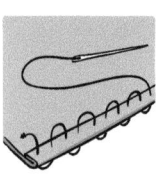

learn

apprendre

work

travailler

marry

se marier

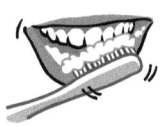

sew

coudre

brush teeth

se brosser les dents

kill

tuer

smoke

fumer

send

envoyer

grandmother
grand-mère

grandfather
grand-père

father
père

mother
mère

baby
bébé

daughter
fille

son
fils

guest

hôte

aunt

tante

uncle

oncle

brother

frère

sister

sœur

body

corps

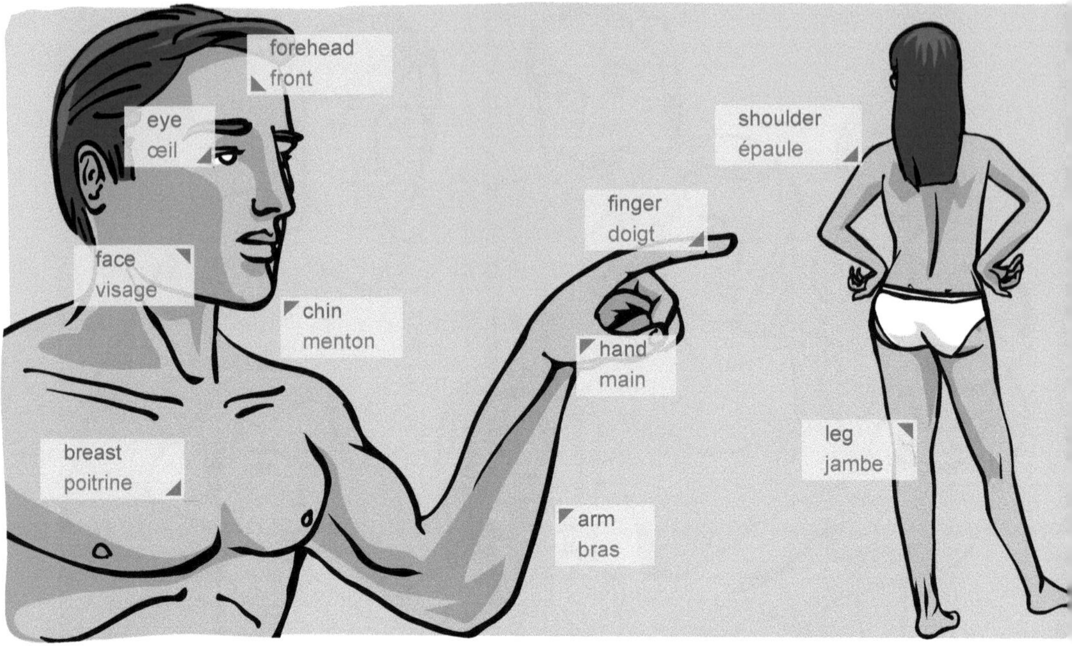

forehead
front

eye
œil

shoulder
épaule

finger
doigt

face
visage

chin
menton

hand
main

breast
poitrine

leg
jambe

arm
bras

baby

bébé

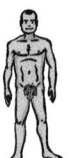

man

homme

woman

femme

girl

fille

boy

garçon

head

tête

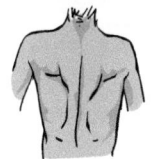

back

dos

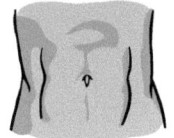

belly

ventre

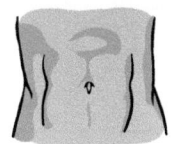

belly button

nombril

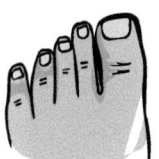

toe

orteil

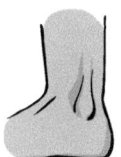

heel

talon

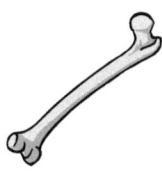

bone

os

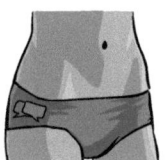

hip

hanche

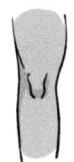

knee

genou

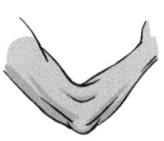

elbow

coude

nose

nez

bottom

fesses

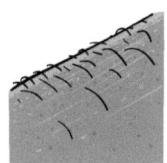

skin

peau

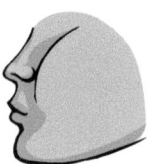

cheek

joue

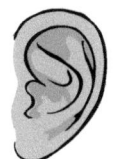

ear

oreille

lip

lèvre

mouth

bouche

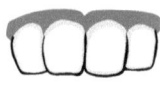

tooth

dent

tongue

langue

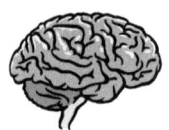

brain

cerveau

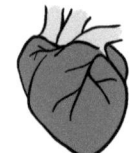

heart

cœur

muscle

muscle

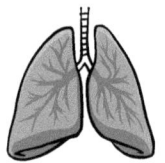

lung

poumons

liver

foie

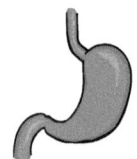

stomach

estomac

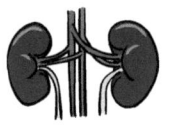

kidneys

reins

sex

rapport sexuel

condom

préservatif

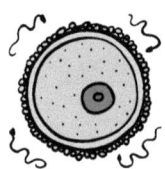

ovum

ovule

semen

sperme

pregnancy

grossesse

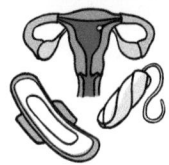

menstruation

menstruation

vagina

vagin

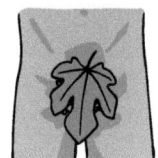

penis

pénis

eyebrow

sourcil

hair

cheveux

neck

cou

hospital
hôpital

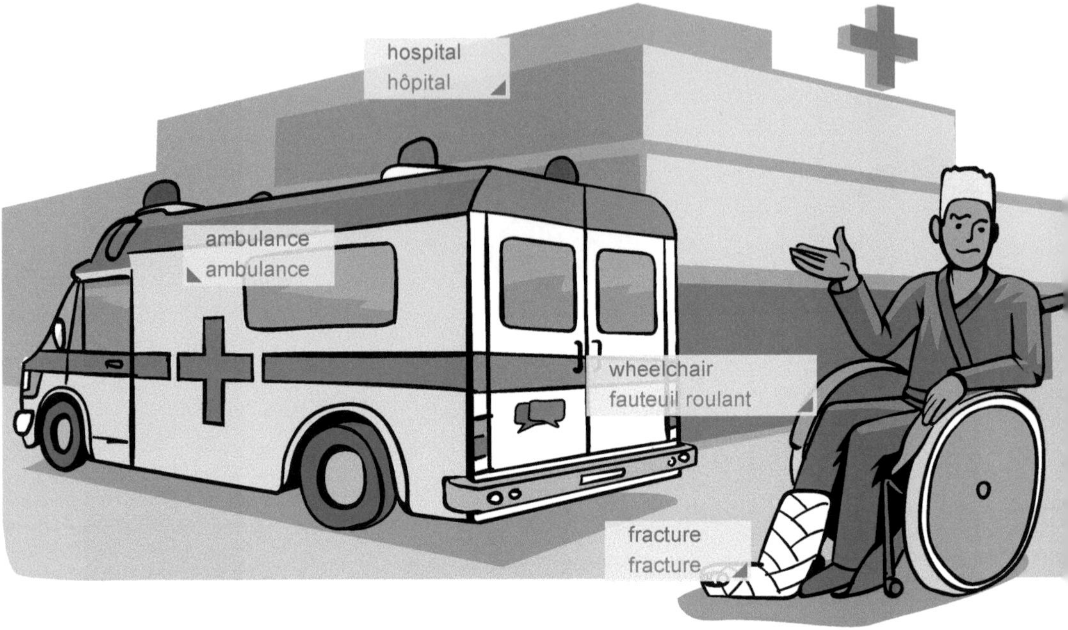

hospital
hôpital
ambulance
ambulance
wheelchair
fauteuil roulant
fracture
fracture

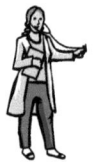

doctor

médecin

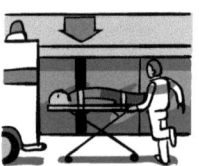

emergency room

service des urgences

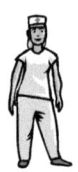

nurse

infirmière

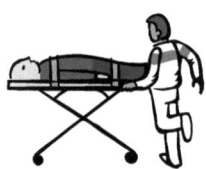

emergency

urgence

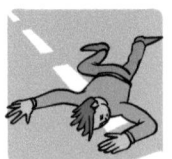

unconscious

inconscient

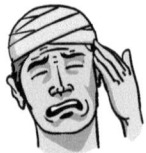

pain

douleur

injury

blessure

bleeding

hémorragie

heart attack

crise cardiaque

stroke

attaque cérébrale

allergy

allergie

cough

toux

fever

fièvre

flu

grippe

diarrhoea

diarrhée

headache

mal de tête

cancer

cancer

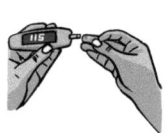

diabetes

diabète

surgeon

chirurgien

scalpel

scalpel

operation

opération

CT

CT

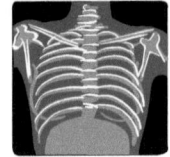

x-ray

radiographie

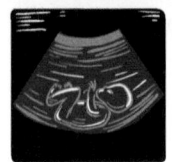

ultrasound

échographie

face mask

masque

disease

maladie

waiting room

salle d'attente

crutch

béquille

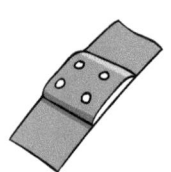

plaster

pansement

bandage

pansement

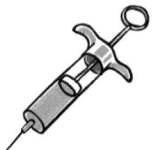

injection

injection

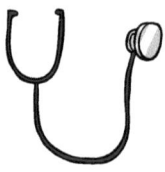

stethoscope

stéthoscope

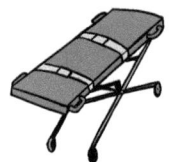

stretcher

brancard

clinical thermometer

thermomètre

birth

accouchement

overweight

surpoids

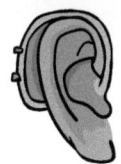

hearing aid

appareil auditif

disinfectant

désinfectant

infection

infection

virus

virus

HIV / AIDS

VIH / sida

medicine

médicament

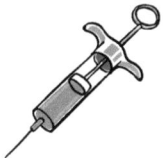

vaccination

vaccination

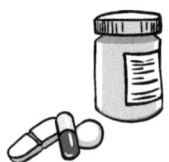

tablets

tablettes

pill

pilule

emergency call

appel d'urgence

blood pressure monitor

tensiomètre

ill / healthy

malade / sain

Help!

Au secours!

alarm

alarme

assault

agression

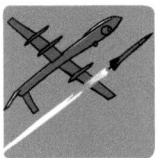

attack

attaque

danger

danger

emergency exit

sortie de secours

Fire!

Au feu!

fire extinguisher

extincteur

accident

accident

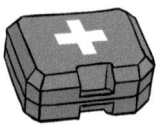

first-aid kit

trousse de premier secours

SOS

SOS

police

police

Europe

Europe

North America

Amérique du Nord

South America

Amérique du Sud

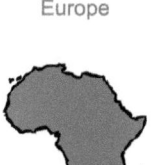

Africa

Afrique

Asia

Asie

Australia

Australie

Atlantic

Océan atlantique

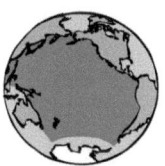

Pacific

Océan pacifique

Indian Ocean

Océan indien

Antarctic Ocean

Océan antarctique

Arctic Ocean

Océan arctique

North Pole

Pônord

Earth - terre

South Pole

Pôsud

Antarctica

Antarctique

Earth

terre

land

pays

sea

mer

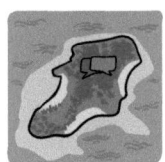

island

île

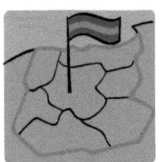

nation

nation

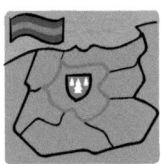

state

état

clock face
....
cadran

hour hand
....
aiguille des heures

minute hand
....
aiguille des minutes

second hand
....
aiguille des secondes

What time is it?
....
Quelle heure est-il?

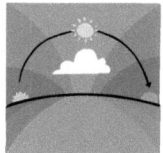

day
....
jour

time
....
temps

now
....
maintenant

digital watch
....
montre digitale

minute
....
minute

hour
....
heure

week

semaine

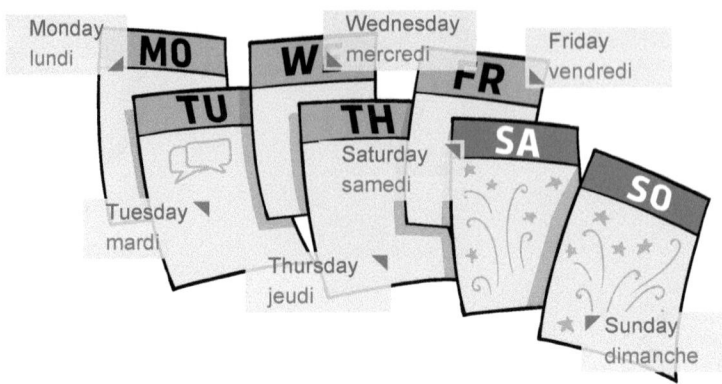

Monday / lundi
Wednesday / mercredi
Friday / vendredi
Tuesday / mardi
Saturday / samedi
Thursday / jeudi
Sunday / dimanche

yesterday

hier

today

aujourd'hui

tomorrow

demain

morning

matin

noon

midi

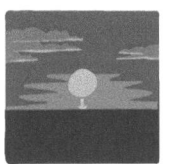

evening

soir

MO	TU	WE	TH	FR	SA	SU
1	2	3	4	5	6	7
8	9	10	11	12	13	14
15	16	17	18	19	20	21
22	23	24	25	26	27	28
29	30	31	1	2	3	4

business days

jours ouvrables

MO	TU	WE	TH	FR	SA	SU
1	2	3	4	5	6	7
8	9	10	11	12	13	14
15	16	17	18	19	20	21
22	23	24	25	26	27	28
29	30	31	1	2	3	4

weekend

week-end

year
année

rain
pluie
spring
printemps
summer
été
wind
vent
autumn
automne
snow
neige
winter
hiver

4.APRIL 11°
5.APRIL 4°
6.APRIL 13°
7.APRIL 8°
8.APRIL 10°

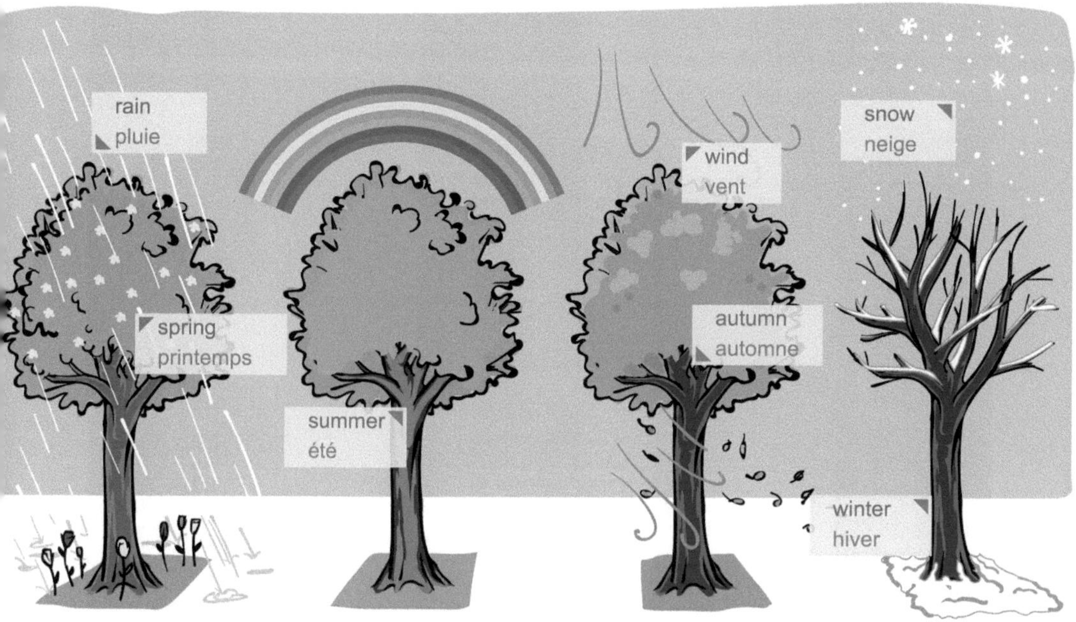

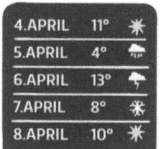

weather forecast

météo

F C
120 40
90 30
60 20
30 10
0 0
-30 -10
-20

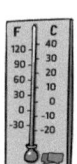

thermometer

thermomètre

sunshine

lumière du soleil

cloud

nuage

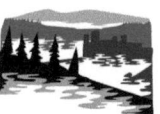

fog

brouillard

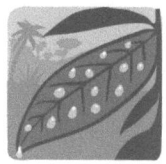

humidity

humidité

lightning

foudre

thunder

tonnerre

storm

tempête

hail

grêle

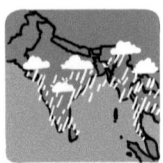

monsoon

mousson

flood

inondation

ice

glace

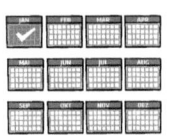

January

janvier

February

février

March

mars

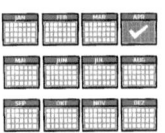

April

avril

May

mai

June

juin

July

juillet

August

août

year - année

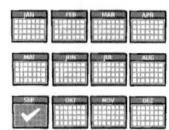

September
....
septembre

October
....
octobre

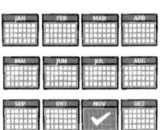

November
....
novembre

December
....
décembre

circle
....
cercle

square
....
carré

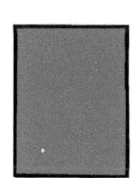

rectangle
....
rectangle

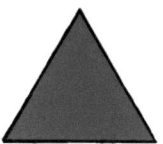

triangle
....
triangle

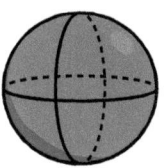

sphere
....
sphère

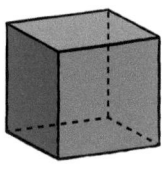

cube
....
cube

white

blanc

yellow

jaune

orange

orange

pink

rose

red

rouge

purple

violet

blue

bleu

green

vert

brown

marron

grey

gris

black

noir

a lot / a little

beaucoup / peu

angry / calm

fâché / calme

beautiful / ugly

joli / laid

beginning / end

début / fin

big / small

grand / petit

bright / dark

clair / obscure

brother / sister

frère / sœur

clean / dirty

propre / sale

complete / incomplete

complet / incomplet

day / night

jour / nuit

dead / alive

mort / vivant

wide / narrow

large / étroit

edible / inedible

comestible / incomestible

evil / kind

méchant / gentil

excited / bored

excité / ennuyé

fat / thin

gros / mince

first / last

premier / dernier

friend / enemy

ami / ennemi

full / empty

plein / vide

hard / soft

dur / souple

heavy / light

lourd / léger

hunger / thirst

faim / soif

ill / healthy

malade / sain

illegal / legal

illégal / légal

intelligent / stupid

intelligent / stupide

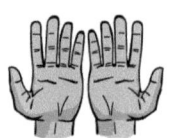

left / right

gauche / droite

near / far

proche / loin

new / used
nouveau / usé

nothing / something
rien / quelque chose

old / young
vieux / jeune

on / off
marche / arrêt

open / closed
ouvert / fermé

quiet / loud
faible / fort

rich / poor
riche / pauvre

right / wrong
correct / incorrect

rough / smooth
rugueux / lisse

sad / happy
triste / heureux

short / long
court / long

slow / fast
lent / rapide

wet / dry
mouillé / sec

warm / cool
chaud / froid

war / peace
guerre / paix

opposites - oppositions

0

zero

zéro

1

one

un

2

two

deux

3

three

trois

4

four

quatre

5

five

cinq

6

six

six

7

seven

sept

8

eight

huit

9

nine

neuf

10

ten

dix

11

eleven

onze

12

twelve

douze

13

thirteen

treize

14

fourteen

quatorze

15

fifteen

quinze

16

sixteen

seize

17

seventeen

dix-sept

18

eighteen

dix-huit

19

nineteen

dix-neuf

20

twenty

vingt

100

hundred

cent

1.000

thousand

mille

1.000.000

million

million

English
anglais

American English
anglais américain

Chinese Mandarin
chinois mandarin

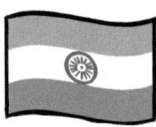

Hindi
hindi

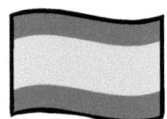

Spanish
espagnol

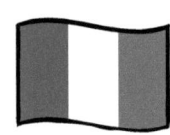

French
français

Arabic
arabe

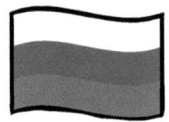

Russian
russe

Portuguese
portugais

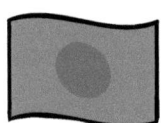

Bengali
bengali

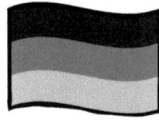

German
allemand

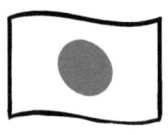

Japanese
japonais

I

je

you

tu

he / she / it

il / elle

we

nous

you

vous

they

ils / elles

who?

qui?

what?

quoi?

how?

comment?

where?

où?

when?

quand?

name

nom

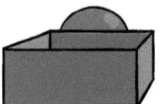

behind

derrière

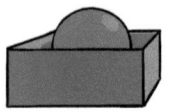

in

dans

in front of

devant

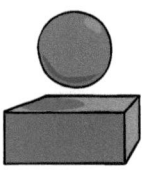

over

au-dessus

on

sur

under

en-dessous

beside

à côté de

between

entre

place

lieu